ISRAEL
FACES AND PLACES

ISRAEL

Presented by GOLDA MEIR

FACES AND PLACES

Photographs by Gemma Levine

G. P. Putnam's Sons New York

For James and Adam

First American Edition 1978
Published by G. P. Putnam's Sons New York

First published in Great Britain by
Weidenfeld and Nicolson Ltd

Library of Congress Catalog Card Number: 78–53457
SBN: 399–12195–1

Printed in Great Britain

Set me as a seal upon thy heart,
As a seal upon thine arm.
For love is strong as death.

from THE SONG OF SONGS

My love affair with Israel really began two years ago. I had visited the country many times before but never had I experienced so profoundly the drama and passion which permeates the land as when I started the photography for this book. Having travelled its length and breadth, I have sought here to portray the rare and delicate beauty of this spiritual, biblical country together with the vivid, endless contrast of its people and landscapes.

The people and the land have endured the torment and desecration of many wars down through the centuries. Standing in the stillness of valleys and deserts that have witnessed battles both ancient and modern, I sensed the awesomeness of the covenant with God which has sustained the Jewish people and reunited them with their homeland. Meeting many Israelis of different backgrounds, races and religions, I discovered a common quality – a spirit and a rare strength which they seem to draw from the ancient, crusted soil. Young people have a surging desire to enjoy life, not to waste it, and wherever I went there was a feeling of togetherness, of warmth and unity.

I was particularly fortunate to be able to share my impressions of Israel with Golda Meir, one of its most respected and beloved leaders. It is a great privilege that she should have agreed to present my work, as someone with a unique involvement in the development of the country, who has helped shape its destiny. I hope that this book will lead others to experience some of the fascination and vibrant beauty of this unique land.

GEMMA LEVINE

There are many people I should thank for making this book possible. In particular I am grateful to George Weidenfeld who commissioned the project. I also must thank my husband Eric who encouraged me throughout the creation of my first book. My gratitude and appreciation also go to Mr Moshe Pearlman, and to General Avraham Yoffee. Finally, I acknowledge the help and assistance of Olympus Cameras and Hasselblad (UK) and Gordon Bishop Associates Limited.

GEMMA LEVINE

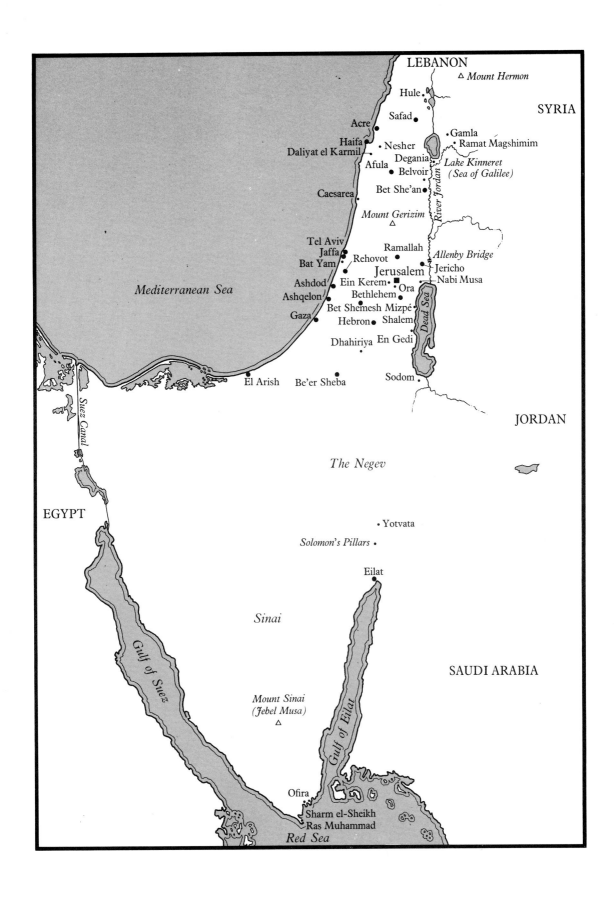

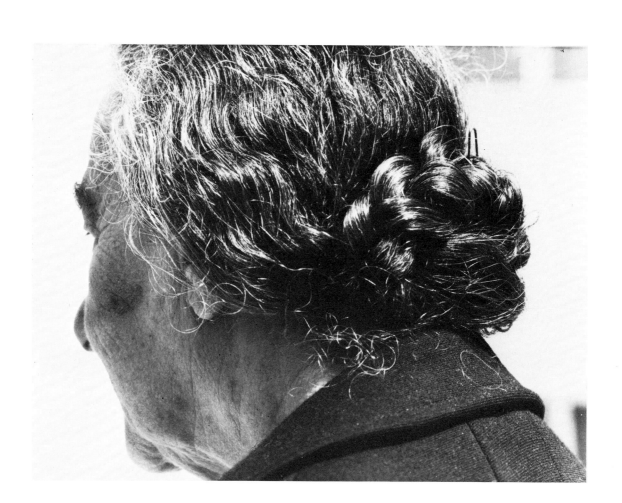

I suppose that nowhere in the world is there quite so small a country as Israel that is quite so packed with history: a few thousand square metres of land that have been fought over, argued about, conquered and freed time and time again – and which, none the less, have always remained in the very centre of consciousness for the Jews who came to it nearly 4,000 years ago, were exiled from it, and have now at last returned to it. In fact, it has been the object of controversy, longing, sacrifice and faith for so many people and for so long that sometimes the great historical issues surrounding it and the bitter battles over it make it hard for non-Israelis to remember that this is also a country in which ordinary people live, bring up children, go shopping, celebrate birthdays, take care of their gardens, quarrel and worry about the weather.

My own Israel, because I have lived in it for well over half a century, is peopled to a large extent by the faces of those who were my comrades in the Labour Zionist struggle to achieve the twin goals of social justice and national independence – and made up of landscapes that my grandchildren might find difficult to identify, even impossible to recognize, but that have retained strong and special associations for me. The little Tel Aviv to which I came in the twenties when I first immigrated to Palestine, the tiny isolated kibbutz in the Galilee in which I worked so happily over fifty years ago, even the long-divided Jerusalem that was my home through much of the fifties and sixties, have all altered enormously under the impact of the sovereign state and its subsequent development and growth, to say nothing of the impact of more recent history.

The land in which I arrived in 1921 was, of course, sparsely populated and terribly neglected. The Jewish community numbered all of 60,000 out of a grand total of 600,000. Tel Aviv was still in its earliest teens, not much more than a large village whose founders – for all of their imagination and optimism – couldn't possibly have imagined that, within the lifetimes of most of them, it would become the largest city in the country, one of the largest in the Middle East. The League of Nations' mandate under which Britain ruled Palestine then – and for another twenty-nine years – had been in force for only a year and Jewish hopes still ran high that the way was now clear for the rebirth of the Jewish National Home. Everything then seemed fresh and full of promise. It was really what Herzl had called it: an old-new land, an amazing combination of ancient sites embedded in the collective memory of the Jews, and of the brave beginnings of an unprecedented national revival. That country, as I experienced it when I first came to it, has remained part of me.

Gemma Levine's Israel, on the other hand, is an Israel seen through the eyes of a young and sensitive artist, and the result is a book that stresses, tenderly and with much talent, Israel's physical loveliness, its human warmth, its basic tolerance and its steadfast belief in a better future for itself and its neighbours, as well as its unbroken involvement with the past. These qualities – not the grim headlines, the perpetual crises, the wars – are what have always made Israel a country unlike any other, and it is therefore entirely appropriate that this reflection of them should appear in the year of the state's thirtieth anniversary.

The North

The Hule Nature Reserve warden and his children 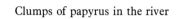 Clumps of papyrus in the river

In the far north of the Jordan Valley lies an area known as the Hule. Originally a vast swampland, plagued by mosquitoes and malaria, teeming with wild life and ablaze with tropical flowers, most of the land, with its good black soil, has been reclaimed from the marsh. Some inhabitants recall the early pioneering days, preserved in songs of the area which tell of the first back-breaking struggles with the swamp. In more recent times, modern drainage equipment has finished the work and now only one corner remains untouched, preserved as a nature reserve.

Planting avocado trees on moshav Gamla

On the strategic Golan Heights, dominating the Jordan Valley, Israel's modern frontier pioneers are building new villages and carving out fields from a harsh terrain. Born to the land, they live and work together in communal settlements (the kibbutzim), or in co-operative settlements (the moshavim). Their clothes mirror their personality and spirit: unconventional, down-to-earth, efficient. They display a healthy streak of romantic idealism – 'With every tree we plant, we give birth', said one – although most would deny it if asked. Whenever another field is cleared of its basalt rocks and a crop planted, they celebrate boisterously with folk-dancing and songs.

Boots of a moshavnik

There are probably few countries as small with a human panorama as vast. Occident and orient meet, though they rarely merge, and often the sole evidence of modern Western culture is a television aerial crazily and improbably planted by a traditional Bedouin tent. Less conservative in all but their distinctive, strict religious beliefs are the Druses of Israel, an old, clannish community that broke away from Islam in the tenth century. Many of the younger generation study and work in Israel's cities while continuing to live in Druse villages.

LEFT Rafik Halabi, a Druse who has become one of
Israel's leading television journalists
BELOW A Bedouin tent in northern Israel

The ruins of Belvoir, which have been partially restored

A cement factory in the industrial suburb of Nesher

Israel is an ancient name and a very modern state. It is
as old as recorded history and as young as the contemporary
independence era, and as a result archaeological sites
jostle with modern developments. At the foot of Mount Gilboa
lies the crusader fortress of Belvoir, which fell to
Saladin in the twelfth century. It is as typical of
the Israeli scenery as is the computerized cement factory
which lies at the foot of Mount Carmel.

Israel is the land of immigrants *par excellence*. In 1948, when the country won its independence, its population was 650,000. Now, it is over 3,000,000. The task of absorbing these people has been formidable for a country so small. It was compounded by the fact that most of the immigrants were penniless refugees from the Middle East countries, or survivors of World War II Nazi concentration camps. When the massive influx was at its height in the early fifties, virtually the whole of Israel was a single refugee camp. Wherever one looked one saw tents and shacks. These have gradually been replaced by suburban apartment estates. Today's immigrants, refugees mainly from the Soviet Union who had to struggle for the right to get out, are provided with temporary dwellings in special absorption centres. Here they learn Hebrew in crash courses, look for work, and generally become acquainted with the country before moving into their permanent homes.

The Russian absorption centre of Ramat Magshimim

A Russian family, outside the house where they have lived for two years

Part of the crypt of St John of Acre

Acre, on the coast of western Galilee, is listed as one of the most ancient
cities in the world. At the time of the biblical Hebrew tribes it was
already an important sea outlet and fishing harbour. Today, Acre is a mixed
town of Jews and Arabs where the old-world crafts are still practised and
where many buildings have borne witness to the excesses of occupying powers,
from Caesar to Napoleon. The crusaders chose Acre as the headquarters
of the Order of the Knights of St John. The surviving crypt stands as
a majestic monument to a once formidable race of conquerors.

A variety of bowls and jugs in an Acre pottery

OVERLEAF Arab head-dresses in an Acre shop window

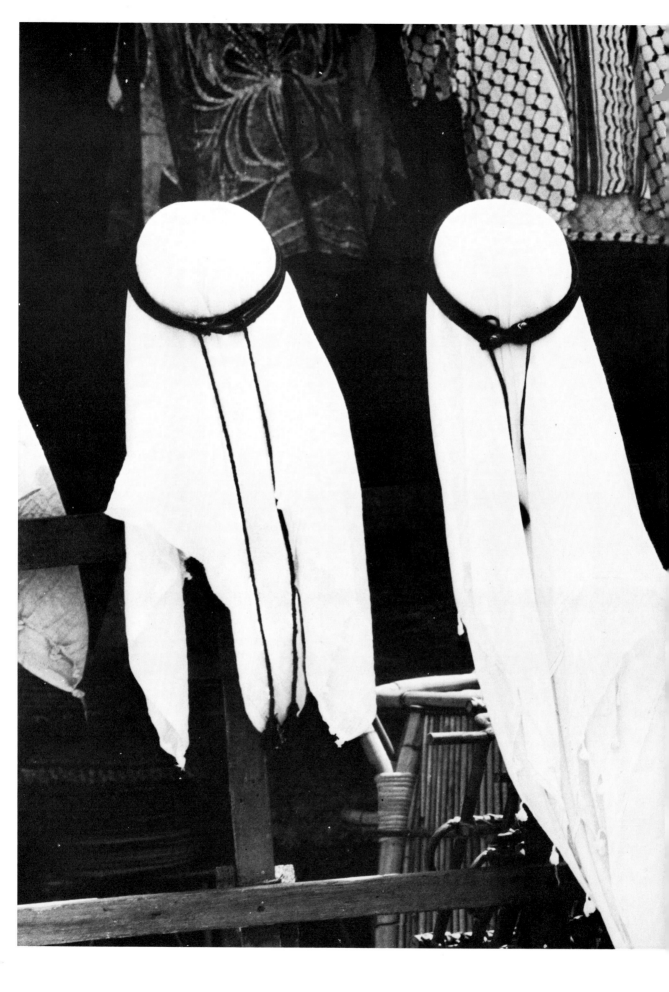

Picking dates on kibbutz Degania

The kibbutz – Hebrew for communal village – is Israel's truly unique contribution to rural development. It is an experiment in voluntary collective living that has worked and increasingly flourished.
The idea was born in 1911, in the eastern Jordan Valley, when a small group of idealists joined together to reclaim the barren, steamy marshland and make it habitable. Necessity compelled them to share everything they owned: to eat together, work together, defend themselves together. The result was kibbutz Degania.

(continued overleaf)

Modern milking equipment in the dairy

Their way of life became the model and the ideal of hundreds of
other pioneers throughout the country. The kibbutz embodied
a renewed relationship of the revived Jewish community with their
land. It is doubtful, indeed, whether the harsh countryside of
desert and marsh, neglected for centuries, could have been
reclaimed were it not for the success of the Degania experiment.
In the ensuing years more than 250 kibbutz villages were

Some of the older generation of kibbutzniks, in the dining-room of kibbutz Degania

established, many of them show-places of garden beauty, advanced industry and agricultural progress. In the history of modern Israel the name 'Degania' persists as the legendary 'Mother' of the kibbutz. Now the fourth generation tends the date palms and the cows whilst the older 'kibbutzniks' can look with some pride upon a flourishing landscape – human and physical – that they helped create with their own bare hands.

Little girls, born and brought up on the kibbutz, play in the fields

There is an ancient Hebrew saying that 'The Land of Israel is acquired only through struggle'. Few areas in the world have witnessed the passing of so many armies, across so many centuries. Certainly, 'struggle' is the incessant theme of the story of Israel's modern rebirth: struggle against nature, against disease, against a 2,000-year exile, against hostile neighbours. Young men – all young men – serve three years in the army, young women two. Reserve duty continues until the age of fifty-five. Soldiering in Israel is rarely a chosen profession; it is a vital national duty unquestionably assumed by a young generation that has never known a day of true peace.

Israeli soldiers in the Golan Heights

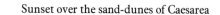
Sunset over the sand-dunes of Caesarea

Blossoming trees against a background of snow-capped mountains.
Mount Hermon, the highest peak, towers over Galilee, only a few hours' drive
from Lake Kinneret, the lowest freshwater source on the earth's surface

Boats on Lake Kinneret (the Sea of Galilee)

OVERLEAF In spring, flowers carpet the hills
overlooking Lake Kinneret

Fishing nets on the quay at the port of Acre

Brightly painted houses in Safad

Children from kibbutz Degania fishing on Lake Kinneret

The Centre

Israel is unique amongst modern nations. Its independence began in 1948, but the origins of the Jewish State are rooted in the pages of the Bible. Two thousand years of exile have intervened since the Roman destruction of Jerusalem in 70 BC, years of wandering, persecution and, a mere generation ago, organized genocide. A strong collective memory of their history has led to a national consensus amongst modern Israelis that no price is too high for the defense of their new home. Never a martial people (their traditional heroes are the prophets and scribes, not the generals), they have been compelled to learn the skills of warfare quickly and efficiently in order to survive. Yet, in an army made up mainly of reservists, from offices and workshops, lecture halls and factories, there is little patience with the rigid, old-fashioned, spit-and-polish approach, and the mobilized student is often the commander of the mobilized teacher. Discipline depends rather on shared convictions and aims.

A soldier on Mount Gerizim, the holy mountain
of the Samaritans

OVERLEAF Army manœuvres in the desert

When there is a mutuality of human interest, sanity prevails. It prevails over two narrow bridges spanning the River Jordan where, by unwritten agreement, tens of thousands of people from Arab countries cross into Israel and the territories it administers. They come to shop, to visit relatives, to tour. A brisk truck traffic carries merchandise and produce, although, as at border crossings throughout the world, there is a need for stringent security precautions. Everything and everybody is searched. Nevertheless, the 'open bridges' across the Jordan River represent common economic and social needs.

LEFT Searching a lorry at the Jordan–Israel border post of Allenby Bridge
BELOW An old lady waits to cross

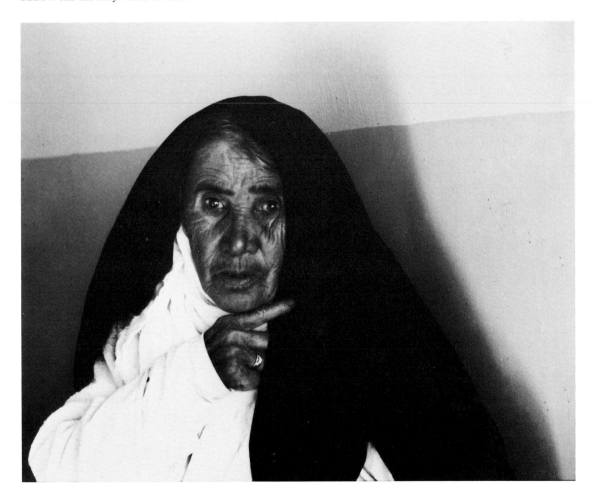

The Patriarch Abraham had two sons, named Isaac and
Ishmael. From the former came the Jewish people,
from the latter, the Arab people. Abraham was renowned
for his hospitality, a quality which has been impressed
on the personality and habits of both lines of his
descendants. The traditional greeting of the one is
'Shalom', of the other, 'Salaam'. Both words mean 'Peace'.

Israeli hospitality: making
coffee for visitors

Old and new buildings in a Tel Aviv street

In 1909, a group of people gathered on a sand-hill by the sea to lay a foundation stone for a new town. They called it Tel Aviv – the Hill of Spring. Now, almost three-quarters of a century later, the town covers many sand-dunes, a spreading metropolis which, together with the towns that have sprung up around it, has almost two million inhabitants: two-thirds of Israel's total population. The city fathers followed the traditional Mediterranean architectural style, of which there are, regrettably, too few examples left.

OVERLEAF Passengers in a bus

Who originally invented the nickname, nobody remembers
or cares, but Israeli-born youth is stuck with it still. They are called
'sabras' – Hebrew for cactus fruits – and, like the fruit
of the cactus, they are ostensibly tough and prickly. But, as
their quick smiles reveal, the toughness is only skin-deep.

Young Israelis: LEFT a motor-cyclist; BELOW in the street, a girl eats falafal
as she talks with a friend

South of Tel Aviv, located in the rural town of Rehovot, is Israel's most
prestigious research centre – the Weizmann Institute of Science. Named after
Chaim Weizmann, the country's first President and himself an eminent scientist,
the Weizmann Institute is one of many research and development units in
the country. Their proliferation reflects the nation's traditional preoccupation
with scholarship and, perhaps more than this, the constant need to overcome
Israel's lack of natural resources and its small size. By an unfortunate trick
of geology, it is one of the few Middle East countries without its own oil;
its wealth must be found instead in the skill of its people.

LEFT AND RIGHT The Weizmann Institute of Science, at Rehovot, near Tel Aviv

It is difficult to say whether there is a distinctive, indigenous
Israeli art style. Each wave of immigrants has added its
own shape to the mould, its own colours to the canvas. The result
is hundreds of galleries and studios exhibiting a wide variety of
styles, schools and experimental work. If there is any connection
at all, it derives, often subtly and sometimes incongruously,
from the Israeli landscape, shaped over the centuries by human
history and the natural sculptors of wind, water and sun.

Samuel Bak, a Polish refugee of World War II,
in the studio where he paints

OVERLEAF Ein Kerem, near Jerusalem, home of many painters
and sculptors, is known as the 'artists' village'

Ira Reichwarger, who emigrated to Israel from
Russia in 1973, with some of her cloth sculptures

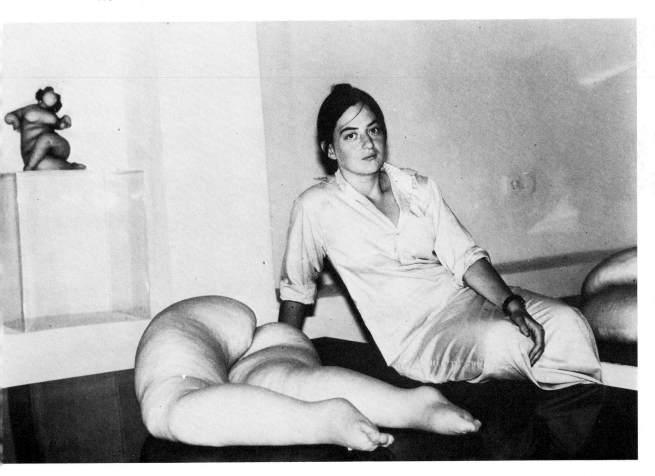

The name 'Israeli' covers a multitude of ethnic identities, and every Israeli street or village reveals faces of arresting character and power. This is particularly true of many older inhabitants, people who, whether they are immigrants or were born here, have experienced convulsive changes during their lifetimes.

LEFT An arresting image of old age and the will to endure: a woman from the Ora mountains who is over a hundred years old
BELOW A Chasid, member of an orthodox Jewish sect

An old man (a Boukharian Jew) keeps careful hold of his chicken in the middle of a busy street

A proud proprietor outside his shop

A bagel kiosk

Selling newspapers from an old pram

As if carved from the living rock, the Greek Orthodox monastery
of Wadi Kelt nestles deep in the mountains of Nabi Musa

There is a road winding eastwards out of Jerusalem whose every
mile is a retreat in time and every curve a century. It skirts
the Old City wall, descends into the Valley of Kidron, touches
the perimeter of Gethsemane, ascends the crest of the Mount of Olives,
twists its way through Bethany and then slopes into the desert,
the Wilderness of Judea. The Wilderness is a wild, dry, empty land which
remains a place for meditation and the search for spiritual truth.

One of the monks

A girl tends her goats on the road to Jericho

A sunset in Jaffa

Tel Aviv, from Jaffa

LEFT Bedouin tents in the North Negev
BELOW A row of decorated camel saddles

LEFT Wild flowers:
(above) silibaum
(below) poppies

RIGHT Cotton fields
near Gaza

A falafal bar in Tel Aviv

Jerusalem

The city of Jerusalem embodies much that lies at the heart of Israel
and its history. A mosaic of ancient and modern buildings, it blends
with the surrounding hillsides from whose rock it has been created.
The stones that built the ancient Temple also built the Hebrew University,
and the city represents the living continuity between twentieth-century
statehood and the Kingdom of David, of which Jerusalem was the capital
nearly 3,000 years ago. Jerusalem's history is not kept behind glass
cases in museums, even though it is now a thriving metropolis of more
than 300,000 people, and few cities can rival its fascination or
personality. The seat of Israel's government, and a place of
scholarship, it also draw pilgrims of many faiths from all over
the world to visit its holy places. Jerusalem is the soul of Israel,
and it lives within its citizens as much as they live within it.

Babies in Hadassah Hospital, Jerusalem

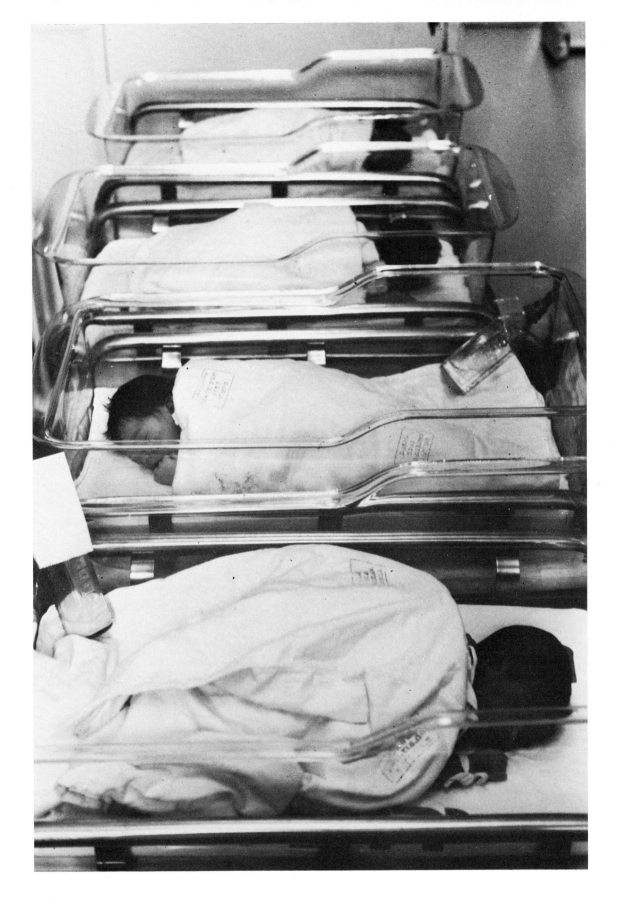

ABOVE The newly built Denmark school in Jerusalem; RIGHT two schoolboys play chess

State-sponsored education is one of Israel's main investments.
In 1948, 141,000 children and young people attended
educational institutions. Today, more than one million
pupils are registered in a wide variety of
schools and colleges. The educational explosion reflects
both the high level of immigration over these thirty
years and the traditional Jewish priority accorded to

(continued overleaf)

education as a value in itself. Almost by definition,
an Israeli school, be it general, religious, comprehensive or vocational,
is more than a place of tuition and learning. It is also a
melting pot for the multi-faceted backgrounds and cultures which
the immigrant children bring with them into the classrooms.
It has taken years of experiment and experience to develop
teaching techniques that successfully integrate the rich
traditions of the immigrant communities with the modern culture
of Israeli society. Israel's pluralistic school life is reflected
by the national youth movements which have always enjoyed
popularity as something more than recreational groups. With an
emphasis on creating good citizens and encouraging volunteer
efforts, they have a strong pioneer tradition, and many young
people from the movements go on to choose the hard but rewarding
life of settlers in Israel's waste places.

Young girls in class

In between lessons, the pupils let off steam and relax with a dance

Students rest against a sculpture by Henry Moore on
the campus of the Hebrew University, Jerusalem

Fourteen per cent – a world record – of the Israeli work force are graduates. The origins of this preoccupation with higher education as the basis for national development dates back to 1912 when much of the country was still marsh and desert. In that year the Technion, Israel's Institute of Technology, was founded in Haifa. Six years later, in 1918, the foundation stone of the Hebrew University in Jerusalem was laid. Since then, six more major institutions of higher learning have been established with branches throughout the country. Israeli university students are, by and large, a pragmatic breed, not given to the kind of volatility that has convulsed western campuses over the past decade. They begin their studies at a relatively late age, after completion of their compulsory military service,

(continued overleaf)

Studying in the sunshine

and are that much older and that much more concerned to complete
their degrees in preparation for civilian life. In addition, the tendency
is to marry young, and most have to work their way through university.
If there is a campus strike, it has more to do with practical matters
such as a rise in fees than with abstract political questions.

In between lectures

It has been said that the Israelis have three national sports: football, basketball and concert-going. Every self-respecting city and many of the large kibbutz villages have their own orchestras or ensembles. The most prestigious is the internationally famous Israel Philharmonic, founded in 1936 by refugees from Nazi Germany, whose first performances were conducted by Toscanini. The Philharmonic's 33,000 subscribers represent a world-record percentage of the population, and its roster includes some of the most eminent conductors and soloists of the musical world.

At a break in rehearsal: instruments of
the Israel Philharmonic Orchestra

Isaac Stern, the world-famous violinist,
and a Russian immigrant

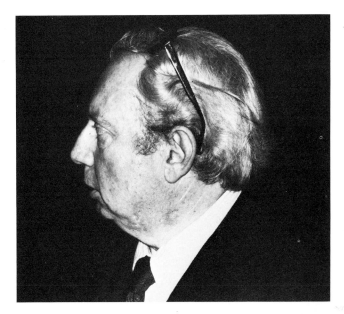

Conductor Zubin Mehta, the present music director of
the orchestra, and of the New York Philharmonic

A glimpse, through a hole in the rocks, of the Jordan Valley

This little boy on a street in Jericho sells freshly-pressed fruit juice.
Oranges are one of Israel's best-known export products

The Samaritans of the famous parable still exist
and worship in modern Israel

ABOVE AND RIGHT A service
in a Greek Orthodox church
in Bethlehem

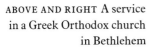

The countryside south of Jerusalem

Ancient tombs in the Kidron Valley

Solomon's Pillars

There is Jerusalem the old, Jerusalem still in its rebuilding and Jerusalem the new. The last is the Jerusalem of public buildings, monuments and parks, many of them still on the drawing board. International experts participate in Jerusalem's planning and architecture, and the result is an increasing number of striking modern buildings.

BELOW The Kennedy Memorial RIGHT Jerusalem's new theatre

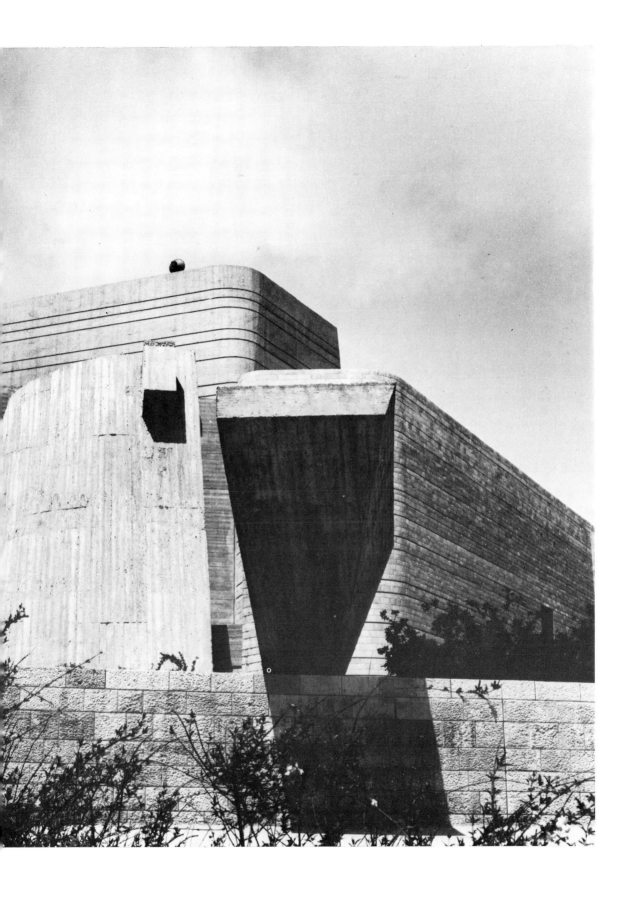

A former Israeli Premier once said that Israel has one Prime Minister and three million aspirants. Politics do indeed play a dominant role in the life of this small nation for whom the stakes are high and the odds great, and a wide scope of opinion is reflected in a variety of political

parties and newspapers. The heart of Israel's democratic life is the Knesset,
the parliament, whose 120 members debate and determine the issues
of the day. The Israeli attitude to government was expressed centuries ago
by Solomon: 'In abundance of counsellors there is safety.'

BELOW Yigael Yadin

RIGHT Moshe Dayan

For more than a century archaeologists have been painstakingly digging
and sifting Jerusalem's terrain. They are continuing even now to uncover
new evidence of the Temple's splendour and its violent destruction,
as well as palace remains and material connected with the origins of
the great monotheistic faiths. There is no part of the country that does not
have some tale to tell, and the meticulous search goes on to discover
traces of former events buried below the earth on which they were enacted.

Excavations in Jerusalem on the Old City wall

Magen Broshi, one of Israel's top archaeologists,
and custodian of the Dead Sea Scrolls

Moshe Safdie is the Israeli architect who won international acclaim for
his 'Habitat '67' design at the World Fair in Montreal. Born in Israel
in 1938, he has lectured all over the world and holds the post of Professor
of Architecture and Director of the Desert Architecture and Environment
Department at Ben Gurion University. Now based in Canada, he is frequently
engaged on work in Israel. He has planned the remodelling of the giant
square of the Temple Western Wall, to give maximum effect to the Wall's

LEFT Moshe Safdie, an architect, in front of the Western Wall
ABOVE In the background, modern buildings designed by Safdie to
blend with the old city remains still being excavated

majestic dimensions and inspirational symbolism; and he has designed
a housing complex within the Jewish quarter of the Old City, integrating
a modern simplicity of shape with the richness of the ancient setting.

A view from the Western Wall of an old part of Jerusalem

ABOVE Two nuns visit the Holy City   RIGHT Two orthodox Jews in the Old City

Jerusalem's religious life is focused on holy places located mainly in
the Old City. Within its few square miles, there are many denominations
of Jews, Christians and Muslims. The inviolability of the shrines and
centres of worship of all faiths, reverently cared for by their traditional
custodians, is guaranteed by law. For Jews, the majority of the community,

(*continued overleaf*)

the holiest of shrines is the Western Wall of the Second Temple.
For Muslims, it is the mosque of Al Aqsa. Christian life in Jerusalem's
Old City, where some 12,000 Christians live, is centred on the Church of
the Holy Sepulchre. By strict historic tradition, the basilica remains under
the custodianship of the Greek Orthodox, the Latin and the Armenian
patriarchs. The Armenian quarter, one of the most prominent in the Old City,
is easily identifiable by the traditional robes of its priests. Every major
denomination, moreover, has its variants and subsects, each clinging
zealously to its distinctive dress and mode of worship. As a result,
the streets of Jerusalem's Old City are a colourful visual reminder
of the possibility of religious co-existence.

LEFT AND RIGHT Greek Orthodox women at prayer

Ornate costumes in an Armenian church service

An Armenian priest

OVERLEAF A typical Jerusalem courtyard

RIGHT An Armenian priest sounds a gong to summon
his congregation to a service
BELOW An old Armenian woman prays in a corner
of the church

The sheep and goat auction held every Thursday morning by
St Stephen's Gate, outside the Old City Wall

Religious co-existence in Jerusalem is a fact. However, the various communities continue to live separately, according to their own traditions and social values, and Jerusalem still has its different 'quarters'. The administration is highly conscious of the difficulties involved in observing such distinctions, while attempting to supervise the city's development and welfare as a whole, and policy on such potentially explosive issues as education demands a high level of consultation and co-operation. Contrary, however, to the tendency in other multi-racial international cities towards integration, a successful future for reunified Jerusalem and its new generation of citizens will probably depend rather on the continuance of voluntary segregation, within a framework of legal equality.

BELOW A fruit and vegetable stall in Mea She'arim, the old Jewish quarter

LEFT AND RIGHT Little boys in the streets of Jerusalem

New apartment blocks, near Jerusalem,
to absorb new immigrants

Teddy Kȯllek, mayor of Jerusalem:
a man of few words, infectious energy,
and a deep sensitivity to the needs and
hopes of Jerusalem and its people

Sunset over Jerusalem

The South

Between the Mountains of Edom in the east and the Wilderness of Judea in the west lies the bottom of the world. Here, in the elongated plain of the southern Jordan Rift Valley, is the Dead Sea, the deepest continental depression on earth, 1,300 feet below the level of the Mediterranean Sea. The River Jordan ends in the Dead Sea's salt-saturated waters, in which nothing but bacteria can live; in the summer, when the air temperature can rise to over 50 °C, the evaporating brine sometimes thickens into an overlying mist which, combined with the rugged surrounding rocks, creates an almost lunar landscape of unearthly beauty. The Dead Sea was the setting for many biblical stories, for example that of Sodom and Gomorrah, the sites of which are now submerged in the southern part of the Sea, and it was in caves on the north-west of the lake that the Dead Sea Scrolls were found, left by early Jewish inhabitants. Now, attempts are being made to reclaim the surrounding land, and the kibbutz at En Gedi has achieved considerable success by the use of modern desalination processes.

The Dead Sea

Down south, in the Arava depression, animals still roam wild as they did
in biblical times. The Yotvata Nature Reserve, an 8,500-acre wildlife game park,
has been developed as an exotic setting of natural beauty for animals like
the oryx, the gazelle and the ibex. The wardens are engaged in attempts
to revive, by controlled breeding, species which were once a common sight,
as many of the Bible's most poetic passages testify. Throughout Israel,
there are some one hundred and twenty areas set aside as nature reserves
in which landscape, flora and fauna receive protection.

General Avraham Yoffee, Director of the Nature Reserves Authority

The white oryx (*Oryx Leucoryx*)

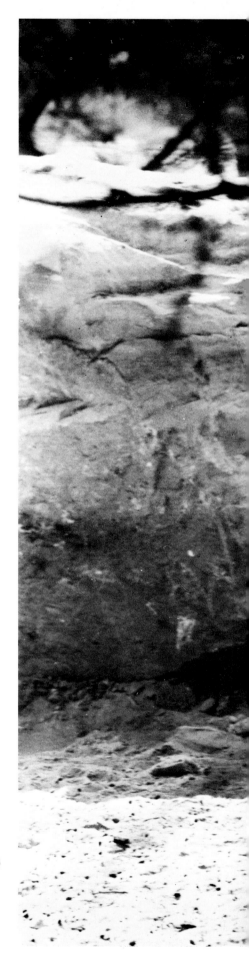

A gazelle from the Negev (*Gazella Dorcas*)

An ibex *(Capra Ibex Nubiana)*

One of the wardens of the Yotvata Nature Reserve

Deep in Israel's southern desert, the Negev, are two human
types – pioneers and Bedouin. The former are locked in
a battle against nature; the latter are at peace with it.
To the one the desert is a place to be tamed and made
green; to the other it is a traditional, unchanging,
vast emptiness to which they have adapted.

Baking pitta, the flat Arab bread

In the heart of the Sinai desert, set in a valley surrounded
by massive cliffs, rests one of the oldest monasteries in
the world, St Catherine's. It stands at the foot of Mount Sinai
and, as the Greek and Arabic inscriptions above the entrance
testify, it was built in the sixth century by the Byzantine
emperor, Justinian. The central chapel is built on the legendary
site of the Burning Bush where God first spoke to Moses.

Waiting for tourists, a little girl begs in the car park
of St Catherine's monastery, on Mount Sinai

The monastery, surrounded by barren, rocky slopes

A little boy in Dhahiriya watches
the world from his window
all day, unable to play
as he has no legs

A gun points across the Dead Sea

The Dead Sea   Pillars of salt in the Dead Sea near
Sodom recall the story of Lot's fate

OVERLEAF The Gulf of Eilat

The mountains of Southern Sinai

The steps of Mount Sinai (Jebel Musa)
which, according to legend, Moses ascended
to receive the Ten Commandments

Sunset over the Dead Sea

The Bedouins (the word comes from the Arabic for 'nomad')
have wandered and grazed the Sinai desert for centuries.
A proud, independent people, they have always resisted attempts
to change or control their lives, although there are
occasional, often incongruous, signs of external influence.

LEFT Silhouetted against the evening sun, a line of Bedouins listen to
a political speech by Yitzhak Rabin, then Prime Minister   BELOW Bedouin faces

The donkey is still a valuable method of transportation
in Israel – in this case, of water

A Bedouin mother and child

The barren wilderness of Sinai has been
a precious possession for different
nations for centuries, simply by virtue
of its geographic position as the bridge
or bulwark between Africa and Asia.
Yet alliances have been forged across
the endless sands, and if peace is to
be achieved in the Middle East, Sinai
is where it will be cemented.

A brief rest in the hot sun for an Israeli soldier

Endless desert, empty
but for two camels on
the distant horizon

The camel has far exceeded any of man's attempts at
adaptation to desert life. Apart from its well-known ability to
exist for several days without water, it has two-toed, flat feet
which enable it to walk or run on sand without sinking.
It also possesses two rows of protective eyelashes, and

(continued overleaf)

the ability to close its nostrils – highly desirable features
in a sand-storm, for which the crude human equivalent
is an enveloping head-dress. Originally wild but now totally
domesticated, the Arabian camel provides transport, wool,
hide, milk and meat.

The camel remains the ideal means of desert transport

Camel footprints in the wind-rippled sand

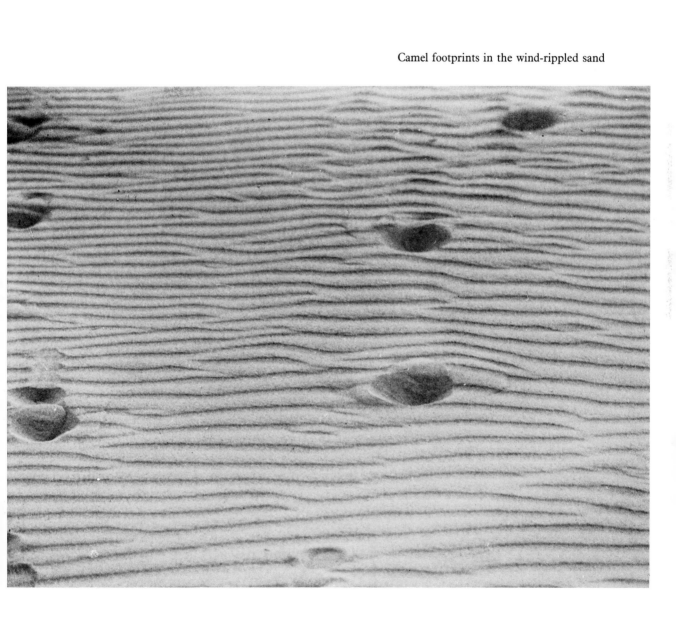

Men, unlike camels, cannot exist without water for
several days, and so gradually new pipelines are
being laid in the desert to bring supplies of sweet
water into a wilderness of few oases and few people.
And yet it was in this same barren wilderness that
Israel's history began, when the human spirit was
witness to six words that were to change human
destiny: 'I am the Lord thy God.' It was this
soldier's ancestors who first heard the Word. With it
the tribes of Israel became the nation of Israel,
a nation that ever since has struggled to survive.
It is a struggle that has brought this young man
back to the very wildnerness where it all began.

A soldier drinks from a sweet water pipe
stretching 100 kilometres from the Gulf of Suez
to the town of Sharm el-Sheikh

The mountains of Southern Sinai